THE SAVORY & SIMPLE KITCHEN

EFFORTLESS RECIPES FOR EVERY MEAL AND EVERY DAY

HENRY M. DIAZ

Copyright © 2025 HENRY M. DIAZ

All rights reserved. No part of this book may be reproduced in any form or by any electronic or mechanical means, including information storage and retrieval systems, without written permission from the author, except for the use of brief quotations in a book review. This book is a work of non-fiction. All views and opinions expressed are those of the author. The author has made every effort to provide accurate information, but does not assume any responsibility for errors or omissions.

DISCLAIMER

Before diving into the delightful world of **_THE SAVORY & SIMPLE KITCHEN_**, please take a moment to read this important information.

General Information

The recipes and tips provided in this cookbook are meant to inspire and guide you in the kitchen. While we've done our best to ensure reliable and practical advice, your results may vary based on factors like ingredient choices, cooking methods, and kitchen equipment. Experimentation is part of the fun, so don't be afraid to adapt recipes to suit your preferences and circumstances.

Health and Safety

Safety first! Cooking is a creative and enjoyable process, but it also comes with risks if proper care isn't taken. Always practice standard kitchen safety:

- Be cautious with sharp knives and utensils.
- Handle hot surfaces, boiling liquids, and heated equipment with care.
- Store perishable ingredients appropriately to avoid spoilage.

Additionally, some ingredients may cause allergic reactions or sensitivities in certain individuals. If you have known food allergies or specific dietary requirements, review each recipe thoroughly before starting. When in doubt, consult with a healthcare provider or nutritionist to ensure the recipes meet your individual needs.

By embracing these precautions and guidelines, you can enjoy the savory simplicity of cooking while ensuring a safe and satisfying experience. Happy cooking!

Nutritional Information

The nutritional information provided for each recipe in _THE SAVORY & SIMPLE KITCHEN_ is an estimate and may vary depending on the specific ingredients, brands, and portion sizes you use. While we've aimed to provide accurate figures, small changes in preparation methods or ingredient choices can lead to variations.

For those seeking more precise nutritional details or needing specific dietary guidance, we recommend consulting a nutritionist or using specialized tools, such as food scales or nutritional analysis apps, to tailor the recipes to your exact needs.

Now that you're ready, let's roll up our sleeves, light up the stove, and bring heart and soul to your table with the savory, simple delights in *THE SAVORY & SIMPLE KITCHEN*.

Enjoy every moment, every recipe, and every bite. Here's to creating meals that nourish and bring joy to your home!

About the Author

Henry M. Diaz is a dedicated culinary enthusiast and recipe innovator with a passion for creating savory dishes that are both flavorful and approachable. With a focus on celebrating the richness of savory cooking, Henry has meticulously developed a collection of recipes that inspire confidence in the kitchen and deliver meals that satisfy both the palate and the soul.

Henry's culinary journey began with a deep desire to simplify the art of cooking while retaining the depth and tradition behind every recipe. Motivated by the joy of sharing meals and creating lasting memories, he has spent years perfecting recipes that embody the balance of simplicity, healthfulness, and indulgence.

As a self-taught chef, Henry understands the challenges of cooking for different skill levels and aims to make every recipe in *The Savory & Simple Kitchen* accessible to all. His philosophy centers around using fresh, wholesome ingredients and straightforward techniques that encourage creativity and success in the kitchen.

Believing that food is a universal language that brings people together, Henry's recipes are designed to foster connection and celebrate the moments shared over a delicious meal. Whether you're cooking for yourself, your family, or entertaining guests, his recipes emphasize the beauty of making everyday meals extraordinary.

In *The Savory & Simple Kitchen*, Henry shares an array of thoughtfully crafted recipes that combine bold flavors, practical tips, and easy-to-follow instructions. From meal planning to savory breakfast, lunch, and dinner ideas, Henry invites readers to explore the art of savory cooking and find joy in every dish. This book is not just a guide to recipes but a celebration of the warmth and satisfaction that only a home-cooked meal can provide.

This book belongs to

_____
_____
_____
_____
_____
_____
_____
_____

Eating well isn't about perfection; it's about giving your body the care it deserves, one delicious bite at a time.

How to Use This Cookbook

This cookbook is your ultimate guide to preparing savory, heartwarming meals that are as easy to make as they are delicious. Whether you're whipping up quick weekday dinners, planning meals for the week ahead, or exploring new ways to bring savory delights to your table, this book is here to support and inspire you. Here's how to make the most of your journey through *The Savory & Simple Kitchen*:

START WITH THE BASICS

If you're new to cooking or simply want to refresh your skills, begin by diving into the introductory chapters. These sections introduce the core principles of savory cooking, guiding you through the essentials:

- Key ingredients to stock in your pantry.
- How to swap ingredients for healthier or more accessible alternatives.
- Tips to create meals that are both nourishing and packed with bold, savory flavors.

Explore Recipes by Meal Type

This cookbook is thoughtfully organized into sections to help you find exactly what you need:

- **Breakfast Recipes:** Start your day with energizing options like savory omelets, breakfast bowls, and hearty baked goods.
- **Lunch Recipes:** Discover balanced and flavorful dishes, such as zesty salads, savory soups, and satisfying grain bowls.
- **Dinner Recipes:** Find everything from quick one-pot meals to rich, slow-cooked dishes perfect for cozy evenings and family gatherings.

Plan Your Week

Meal planning is made simple with this cookbook! You'll find tips and strategies to help you:

- Create weekly meal plans using recipes from each section.

- Prep ingredients ahead of time for easy assembly during busy days.
- Mix and match recipes to suit your schedule and preferences.
  Many recipes also include prep-ahead instructions, so you can save time and enjoy home-cooked meals without the stress.

Understand the Recipe Format

Every recipe in this book is crafted to make cooking approachable and enjoyable. Here's what each recipe includes:

- **Ingredients List:** A selection of wholesome, easy-to-find ingredients that maximize flavor.
- **Prep Time & Cook Time:** To help you plan your meals efficiently.
- **Step-by-Step Instructions:** Clear and concise directions to guide you through every step of the cooking process.
- **Pro Tips:** Handy advice for enhancing flavors, adjusting recipes to your liking, or simplifying preparation.
- **Storage and Reheating Notes:** Guidance on keeping your meals fresh and reheating them to perfection.

Customize Recipes to Fit Your Taste

Cooking is about creativity! Each recipe is designed to be flexible, allowing you to:

- Adjust ingredients to fit your personal taste or dietary preferences.
- Experiment with different vegetables, proteins, or seasonings.
- Put your unique spin on classic dishes, making them your own.

Incorporate Healthy Choices

This cookbook emphasizes meals that are as good for your health as they are satisfying. Throughout the recipes, you'll find tips to:

- Lighten up dishes without compromising flavor.
- Add nutritional value with simple ingredient swaps.
- Maintain a balance of indulgence and nourishment in every meal.

Embrace the Special Sections

The Savory & Simple Kitchen is more than a recipe book—it's a resource for creating a lifestyle centered around delicious and wholesome food. Be sure to explore:

- **Meal Planning Tips:** Learn how to stock your kitchen with essentials, streamline your grocery shopping, and simplify your cooking routine.
- **Savory Cooking Principles:** Master the techniques that make savory dishes so satisfying and flavorful.

With *The Savory & Simple Kitchen*, you'll discover how eay and enjoyable it can be to bring flavorful, hearty meals to your table every day. Let's get cooking and make every moment in the kitchen an adventure worth savoring!

Troubleshooting Guide

Cooking isn't always perfect, but that's part of the adventure! In *The Savory & Simple Kitchen*, we've got you covered with answers to common challenges and tips to help you adjust as you go:

- **Balancing Your Plate:** Learn how to create meals that are both satisfying and nutritionally balanced by incorporating a variety of proteins, vegetables, and grains.
- **Troubleshooting Recipes:** From dishes that didn't turn out as expected to adjusting seasoning or consistency, you'll find practical advice to save the day and make the most of your ingredients.

Tips for Hosting

Whether you're hosting an intimate dinner or a lively gathering, this cookbook includes ideas to ensure your meals are both memorable and manageable. Discover:

- Recipes that are crowd-pleasers and easy to prepare in advance.
- How to cater to various dietary preferences while keeping everyone happy.
- Strategies for serving meals that feel special without added stress.

Learn as You Go

Cooking is a skill that develops over time, and *The Savory & Simple Kitchen* is designed to grow with you. If you're new to the kitchen or looking to boost your confidence, start with simpler recipes and gradually explore more advanced techniques. This cookbook emphasizes understanding the joy of food and the comfort it brings, so you can make every dish meaningful.

Share the Experience

Food is about connection, whether you're enjoying a solo dinner or gathering with loved ones. Share your meals and the joy of cooking with those around you. Found a recipe you adore? Make it your own by adding personal twists and share your creations with friends and family—it's the best way to spread the love for savory cooking.

Enjoy the Journey

The Savory & Simple Kitchen is your guide to crafting meals that bring warmth, satisfaction, and joy to your table. Whether you're a seasoned chef or a beginner, this book aims to inspire you to cook with love, creativity, and confidence.

So, gather your ingredients, choose a recipe that excites you, and let's dive into a world of delicious, heartwarming savory meals. Your culinary adventure starts here—enjoy every moment, every flavor, and every bite!

Table of Contents

Introduction 14
   Why Savory? 14
   What to Expect 14
   A Book for Every Cooks 15

How to Start and Stick to Savory Recipes 16
   Step 1: Understand What "Savor" Means 16
   Step 2: Start Simple 16
   Step 3: Stock Your Savory Toolkit 17
   Step 4: Build a Routine 17
   Step 5: Embrace Mistake 17
   Step 6: Celebrate Your Win 18
   Stayig Inspired 18

Foods to Eat and Avoid for a Healthy Savory Lifestyle 22
   Foods to Eat 22
   Foods to Avoid 23
   Final Thoughts 24
   Questions 25

Meal Planning for Beginner Savory Recipes 26
   1. Start with a Goal 26
   2. Plan Around Your Schedule 26

3. Choose Simple, Versatile Recipes 26

4. Build a Balanced Plate 27

5. Make a Grocery List 27

6. Prep Ahead of Time 27

7. Keep It Flexible 28

8. Evaluate and Adjust 28

A Beginner-Friendly Example Plan 28

7-Day Savory Recipes Meal Plan 30

Day 1: 30

Day 2: 30

Day 3: 31

Day 4: 32

Day 5: 32

Day 6: 33

Day 7: 34

Tips for the Meal Plan: 34

7 Savory Breakfast Recipes 35

Savory Scrambled Eggs with Spinach and Feta 36

Avocado Toast with Egg and Sriracha 37

Vegetable Omelet with Mushrooms, Bell Peppers, and Cheddar 38

Savory Oatmeal with Avocado and Poached Egg 39

Shakshuk (Poached Eggs in Spicy Tomato Sauce) 40

Savory Breakfast Burrito 41

Egg and Veggie Breakfast Bowl 42

Savory Lunch Recipes 43

Grilled Chicken and Avocado Salad 44

Quinoa Salad with Roasted Vegetables and Lemon Dressing 45

Lentil Soup with Carrots and Celery 46

Turkey and Avocado Lettuce Wraps 47

Salmon and Roasted Brussels Sprouts Salad 48

Chickpea and Tomato Stew 49

Egg Salad with Roasted Sweet Potatoes 50

Savory Dinner Recipes 51

Garlic Butter Shrimp and Asparagus 52

Baked Lemon Herb Chicken Thighs 53

Spaghetti Squash with Marinara Sauce and Turkey Meatballs 54

Beef Stir-Fry with Vegetables 55

Stuffed Bell Peppers with Quinoa and Ground Beef 56

beef Tenderloin with Roasted Root Vegetables 57

Vegetarian Chili 58

Conclusion 59

INTRODUCTION

Welcome to *The Savory & Simple Kitchen*, where the art of crafting flavorful, satisfying meals meets the ease of practical cooking. Whether you're a seasoned chef with a passion for bold flavors or a curious beginner ready to embark on your culinary journey, this book is your ultimate guide to mastering the savory recipes lifestyle.

Savory cooking is more than just a method; it's a celebration of taste, a symphony of aromas, and the heart of meals that bring people together. It's about embracing the rich, deep, and umami-filled flavors that elevate everyday ingredients into unforgettable dishes. But it's also about simplicity—because great food doesn't have to be complicated. In fact, the best recipes are those that balance ease and excellence.

WHY SAVORY?

Savory cooking is for everyone. It's about dishes that warm your soul, meals that nourish your body, and flavors that linger in your memory long after the last bite. It's the comforting smell of garlic sizzling in olive oil, the transformative power of a perfectly balanced marinade, and the joy of a crispy crust giving way to a tender interior.

For the novice, this book will guide you through the basics, from understanding key ingredients to mastering foundational techniques. For the experienced cook, it offers new twists on classics, creative recipes to expand your repertoire, and tips to enhance your skills.

WHAT TO EXPECT

Inside these pages, you'll find more than just recipes. You'll discover tools for success in every savory dish you create:

- **Meal Planning Made Simple**: Learn how to plan meals that save time, reduce waste, and ensure every bite is as delicious as it is satisfying.
- **Essential Cooking Tips**: From choosing the freshest ingredients to understanding the science of seasoning, we'll cover the secrets to perfecting every dish.

- **Recipes for Every Occasion**: Dive into curated chapters for breakfast, lunch, and dinner, each packed with savory delights ranging from quick weekday meals to indulgent weekend feasts.
- **A Savory Mindset**: Build the habits and skills to stay consistent, motivated, and confident in your cooking journey.

A BOOK FOR EVERY COOK

This book isn't about rigid rules or intimidating techniques. It's about empowering you to embrace the joy of cooking savory meals, one recipe at a time. Whether you're crafting a hearty stew on a chilly evening, perfecting the art of a crisp pan-seared chicken, or experimenting with bold spices in a new recipe, you'll feel guided and inspired every step of the way.

So, let's tie on our aprons, grab our favorite pans, and dive into the world of savory cooking. Together, we'll make your kitchen the heart of unforgettable meals and lasting memories.

Welcome to *The Savory & Simple Kitchen*. Let's get cooking!

HOW TO START AND STICK TO SAVORY RECIPES

Starting a journey into savory cooking is like opening the door to a world of mouthwatering possibilities. It's exciting, a little daunting, and absolutely worth it. Whether you're looking to level up your cooking game or simply add more variety to your meals, learning how to prepare savory recipes will keep your taste buds happy and your kitchen lively.

But let's be real—starting something new is one thing; sticking with it is another. Life gets busy, ingredients go bad, and sometimes, you just don't feel like cooking. That's okay! This chapter is here to help you navigate the ups and downs of your savory cooking adventure with practical tips, encouragement, and a dose of real talk.

STEP 1: UNDERSTAND WHAT "SAVOR" MEANS

Let's start with the basics: savory cooking is all about depth of flavor. Think of dishes that make you pause after the first bite because they're just that good. It's the perfect balance of salt, herbs, spices, and umami—the savory "fifth taste" that makes food irresistible.

Here's the good news: you don't need fancy ingredients or years of experience to create savory meals. You just need the right mindset and a willingness to experiment.

STEP 2: START SIMPLE

No one becomes a master overnight, and that's okay. Starting small is key to building confidence in the kitchen.

- **Master a Few Basics**: Focus on a handful of simple recipes that highlight savory flavors, like roasted vegetables, a hearty soup, or a stir-fry with garlic and soy sauce. These dishes will introduce you to layering flavors without overwhelming you.
- **Get Comfortable with Spices**: Start with staples like garlic powder, paprika, cumin, and dried herbs like thyme or oregano. Once you're confident, experiment with blends like curry powder or smoked chili.

Think of these early recipes as your training wheels. They're delicious on their own, but they'll also teach you the fundamentals for tackling more complex dishes later.

STEP 3: STOCK YOUR SAVORY TOOLKIT

A well-stocked kitchen makes cooking feel less like a chore and more like an adventure. Here's what you need:

1. **Flavor Bombs**: Stock up on essentials like soy sauce, miso paste, fish sauce, balsamic vinegar, and Worcestershire sauce. These ingredients add that magical savory punch.
2. **Herbs & Spices**: Fresh herbs like parsley and cilantro add brightness, while spices like cumin, coriander, and smoked paprika add depth.
3. **Broths & Stocks**: These are the backbone of soups, stews, and sauces. Always have some on hand—store-bought is fine, but homemade is even better!
4. **Pantry Staples**: Think canned tomatoes, lentils, pasta, rice, and beans. These can be transformed into endless savory meals with a few added ingredients.

STEP 4: BUILD A ROUTINE

Let's face it—consistency is the hardest part. But sticking to savory recipes doesn't mean spending hours in the kitchen every day. It's about creating a routine that works for you.

- **Set a Goal**: Maybe it's cooking one savory meal per week or making dinner at home four nights out of seven. Start small and build up as you gain confidence.
- **Meal Prep Like a Pro**: Pick a day to prep ingredients or cook in bulk. Roast vegetables, cook grains, or marinate proteins in advance so weeknight cooking feels effortless.
- **Make It Social**: Invite friends or family over for a savory dinner. Sharing your creations is one of the most rewarding parts of cooking.

STEP 5: EMBRACE MISTAKE

Let me tell you a secret: even the best cooks mess up. You'll burn the garlic sometimes. You'll over-salt the soup. You'll forget the timer and find your roast a little crispier than planned. And you know what? That's okay. Every mistake is a lesson in disguise.

When something doesn't turn out the way you hoped, ask yourself: What could I do differently next time? Maybe you'll discover that garlic burns quickly at high heat or that your taste buds prefer a lighter hand with soy sauce. Either way, you're learning—and that's what matters.

STEP 6: CELEBRATE YOUR WIN

Every dish you make is an achievement. Celebrate it! Made a perfectly creamy risotto? That's worth a toast. Finally figured out how to get your chicken crispy and juicy? High five yourself.

Don't compare your progress to anyone else's. Your journey with savory cooking is uniquely yours.

STAYIG INSPIRED

Cooking savory meals is a lifelong adventure. There's always something new to try, whether it's a bold recipe from a different culture or a twist on an old favorite. Keep exploring, stay curious, and let your taste buds lead the way.

Remember, this journey isn't about perfection—it's about enjoying the process. So grab your spatula, turn on some music, and let the magic happen in *The Savory & Simple Kitchen*. You've got this!

1. **"What's your go-to savory dish, and how would you elevate it with a new ingredient or technique?"**
   Let's explore how even a simple dish can become extraordinary with small tweaks—like adding smoked paprika to roasted veggies or finishing a soup with a splash of balsamic vinegar.
2. **"If you could stock only five pantry staples for savory cooking, which ones would you choose and why?"**
   This is a fun way to think critically about building a versatile pantry. I'd love to share my top picks and why they're must-haves in my kitchen.
3. **"What's the most intimidating part of starting a new recipe for you, and how can we break it down into manageable steps?"**

Cooking doesn't have to feel overwhelming! Let's tackle those fears together—whether it's handling new ingredients or mastering a tricky technique.

4. **"Have you ever tried a savory dish that completely changed the way you think about food? What was it?"**

   Stories about food are powerful. They connect us to experiences and cultures. Let's talk about that unforgettable first bite and how it can inspire your cooking.

5. **"What's one mistake you've made in the kitchen that turned out to be a valuable lesson?"**

   We all have those moments where things go sideways—but they often teach us the most. Share your story, and I'll share one of mine to keep us motivated!

QUESTIONS

What's your go-to savory dish, and how would you elevate it with a new ingredient or technique?

If you could stock only five pantry staples for savory cooking, which ones would you choose and why?

What's the most intimidating part of starting a new recipe for you, and how can we break it down into manageable steps?

Have you ever tried a savory dish that completely changed the way you think about food? What was it?

What's one mistake you've made in the kitchen that turned out to be a valuable lesson?

FOODS TO EAT AND AVOID FOR A HEALTHY SAVORY LIFESTYLE

The savory cooking lifestyle is all about enjoying rich, flavorful meals that nourish the body and soul. But to stay healthy while indulging in these bold flavors, it's essential to choose your ingredients wisely. Let's dive into the foods to embrace and those to steer clear of to maintain a balanced and nutritious diet.

FOODS TO EAT

1. **Fresh Vegetables**
   - **Why:** Vegetables are the backbone of healthy savory meals, offering vitamins, minerals, and fiber while being low in calories.
   - **Best Choices:** Leafy greens, bell peppers, zucchini, mushrooms, broccoli, carrots, tomatoes, and eggplants.
   - **Tips:** Roast them for added depth, sauté with garlic for a quick side, or blend into soups for creamy goodness without cream.

2. **Lean Proteins**
   - **Why:** Proteins like chicken, fish, and plant-based options provide essential amino acids to keep your body strong and energized.
   - **Best Choices:** Skinless chicken, turkey, salmon, tuna, tofu, tempeh, lentils, and chickpeas.
   - **Tips:** Marinate proteins to infuse flavor without extra calories. Grilling, baking, or steaming preserves their nutritional value.

3. **Whole Grains**
   - **Why:** They are a great source of fiber, complex carbohydrates, and essential nutrients.
   - **Best Choices:** Brown rice, quinoa, farro, bulgur, and whole-grain bread or pasta.

- o **Tips:** Use whole grains as a base for stir-fries, salads, or grain bowls for a satisfying, savory meal.
4. **Healthy Fats**
    - o **Why:** Fats like those found in olive oil and avocados are essential for brain function and overall health.
    - o **Best Choices:** Extra virgin olive oil, avocado, nuts, seeds, and fatty fish like salmon or mackerel.
    - o **Tips:** Drizzle olive oil over roasted vegetables, or add avocado slices to your meals for creamy richness.
5. **Flavor Enhancers**
    - o **Why:** Herbs, spices, and natural flavor boosters enhance taste without relying on unhealthy additives.
    - o **Best Choices:** Garlic, onion, ginger, fresh herbs, spices like cumin or smoked paprika, and umami-rich ingredients like miso or nutritional yeast.
    - o **Tips:** Experiment with spice blends or fresh herb combinations to create signature flavors for your dishes.

FOODS TO AVOID

1. **Processed Meats**
    - o **Why:** These often contain high levels of sodium, unhealthy fats, and preservatives, which can harm long-term health.
    - o **Examples:** Bacon, sausages, deli meats, and hot dogs.
    - o **Alternative:** Opt for grilled or roasted lean cuts of meat instead.
2. **Refined Carbohydrates**
    - o **Why:** Foods like white bread, white rice, and pastries lack fiber and can cause blood sugar spikes.
    - o **Examples:** White flour products, sugary cereals, and packaged snacks.
    - o **Alternative:** Swap these for whole-grain or high-fiber versions.
3. **High-Sodium Foods**

- o **Why:** Excess sodium can lead to high blood pressure and other health issues.
- o **Examples:** Store-bought sauces, canned soups, processed snacks, and salty condiments like soy sauce.
- o **Alternative:** Choose low-sodium or make homemade versions of sauces and broths.

4. **Unhealthy Fats**
   - o **Why:** Trans fats and excessive saturated fats increase the risk of heart disease.
   - o **Examples:** Margarine, fried foods, and processed baked goods.
   - o **Alternative:** Use healthy fats like olive oil or avocado for cooking and avoid frying foods when possible.

5. **Sugar-Loaded Ingredients**
   - o **Why:** Hidden sugars in sauces, marinades, and dressings can sabotage an otherwise healthy dish.
   - o **Examples:** Sweetened ketchup, teriyaki sauce, and bottled dressings.
   - o **Alternative:** Opt for homemade dressings and marinades with natural sweeteners like honey or none at all.

FINAL THOUGHTS

A healthy savory lifestyle is about balance. Focus on whole, unprocessed ingredients that pack a punch in flavor and nutrients, and minimize the foods that detract from your health goals. By making thoughtful choices, you can enjoy the bold and satisfying world of savory cooking while keeping your body happy and healthy.

QUESTIONS

1. Which of the following is NOT recommended as part of a healthy savory cooking lifestyle?

    a) Fresh vegetables like broccoli and zucchini

    b) Lean proteins such as salmon and tofu

    c) Processed meats like bacon and hot dogs

    d) Whole grains like quinoa and brown rice

2. What is a healthy alternative to high-sodium store-bought sauces?

    a) Bottled dressings with added sugar

    b) Homemade sauces and marinades

    c) Canned soups

    d) Teriyaki sauce

3. Which of the following is a key component of a balanced savory meal?

    a) Trans fats from margarine

    b) Refined carbohydrates like white bread

    c) Healthy fats such as olive oil and avocado

    d) High-sodium processed snacks

Answer: c) Processed meats like bacon and hot dogs

Answer: b) Homemade sauces and marinades

Answer: c) Healthy fats such as olive oil and avocado

MEAL PLANNING FOR BEGINNER SAVORY RECIPES

Meal planning can be a game-changer for anyone new to savory cooking. It saves time, reduces stress, minimizes waste, and ensures you always have delicious, balanced meals ready to go. The key is to keep it simple, organized, and tailored to your preferences. Here's how to get started:

1. START WITH A GOAL

Before you dive into planning, decide on your purpose:

- Are you cooking to save time during the week?
- Do you want to eat healthier, more balanced meals?
- Are you experimenting with new savory recipes?

Having a clear goal helps you stay focused and motivated.

2. PLAN AROUND YOUR SCHEDULE

Be realistic about your time. Ask yourself:

- How many meals do you need to plan for?
- Do you have busy days where quick recipes are best?
- Can you dedicate a weekend afternoon to prep for the week?

For beginners, start with planning 3–5 meals per week, leaving room for leftovers or spontaneous dinners.

3. CHOOSE SIMPLE, VERSATILE RECIPES

As a beginner, focus on savory recipes that:

- Use a few basic ingredients.

- Don't require advanced techniques.
- Can be easily adapted (e.g., roasted vegetables, stir-fries, soups).

Examples:

- Garlic and herb roasted chicken with vegetables.
- A hearty lentil and vegetable soup.
- Quick stir-fried beef or tofu with soy sauce and ginger.

4. BUILD A BALANCED PLATE

A well-planned savory meal is both nutritious and satisfying. Aim for:

- **Protein:** Chicken, fish, tofu, lentils, or eggs.
- **Vegetables:** At least half your plate with a mix of colors and textures.
- **Grains or Carbs:** Brown rice, quinoa, or roasted sweet potatoes.
- **Healthy Fats:** Drizzle olive oil, sprinkle nuts, or add avocado.

5. MAKE A GROCERY LIST

Write down all the ingredients you'll need for the week. To stay organized:

- Group items by category (produce, proteins, pantry staples, etc.).
- Check your kitchen to avoid buying duplicates.

Tip: Stick to your list to save money and reduce impulse buys.

6. PREP AHEAD OF TIME

Spend a little time prepping ingredients or meals in advance:

- **Chop Vegetables:** Store them in airtight containers for easy use.
- **Cook Staples:** Boil grains, roast vegetables, or grill proteins for quick assembly.
- **Batch Cook:** Make a big pot of soup, stew, or sauce to enjoy over multiple meals.

Example: Roast a large tray of vegetables and chicken thighs on Sunday. Use them throughout the week in salads, wraps, or grain bowls.

7. KEEP IT FLEXIBLE

Meal planning doesn't mean locking yourself into a rigid schedule. Life happens, and cravings change! Build some flexibility into your plan:

- Swap meals if your mood changes.
- Use leftovers creatively (e.g., turn roasted veggies into a frittata).
- Keep a few quick, no-cook options on hand, like a savory salad or sandwich.

8. EVALUATE AND ADJUST

After your first week of meal planning, reflect on what worked and what didn't:

- Did you enjoy the recipes?
- Were the portions right?
- Was the prep manageable?

Use what you learn to refine your plan for the next week.

A BEGINNER-FRIENDLY EXAMPLE PLAN

Day 1:

- **Dinner:** Garlic and herb roasted chicken with sweet potatoes and steamed broccoli.

Day 2:

- **Lunch:** Leftover chicken in a savory salad with mixed greens, avocado, and balsamic dressing.
- **Dinner:** Lentil and vegetable soup with whole-grain bread.

Day 3:

- **Lunch:** Quick stir-fried tofu with soy sauce, ginger, and sautéed vegetables over brown rice.
- **Dinner:** Sheet pan roasted salmon with asparagus and quinoa.

Day 4:

- **Lunch:** Savory sandwich with leftover salmon, cucumber, and a dill yogurt sauce.
- **Dinner:** Pasta tossed with garlic, olive oil, cherry tomatoes, and fresh basil.

Day 5:

- **Lunch:** Leftover pasta with added sautéed spinach and mushrooms.

By planning ahead, you'll find that savory cooking becomes a joyful and stress-free part of your week. Happy cooking!

7-DAY SAVORY RECIPES MEAL PLAN

This meal plan is designed for beginners, focusing on simplicity, flavor, and balance. Each meal is easy to prepare, nutrient-dense, and loaded with savory goodness. The plan includes a mix of protein, vegetables, grains, and healthy fats to keep you satisfied throughout the week. Feel free to swap out ingredients based on your preferences or what's in season.

DAY 1:

Breakfast:

- **Savory Scrambled Eggs with Spinach and Feta**
  Scramble eggs with sautéed spinach, onions, and a sprinkle of feta cheese. Serve with a slice of whole-grain toast.

Lunch:

- **Chicken and Avocado Salad**
  Grilled chicken breast, mixed greens, cucumber, cherry tomatoes, and avocado, drizzled with olive oil and balsamic vinegar.

Dinner:

- **Garlic and Herb Roasted Chicken with Sweet Potatoes and Steamed Broccoli**
  Marinate chicken thighs with garlic, rosemary, olive oil, and lemon. Roast with diced sweet potatoes and broccoli.

DAY 2:

Breakfast:

- **Savory Oatmeal with Avocado and Poached Egg**
  Cook oats in low-sodium vegetable broth and top with sliced avocado, a poached egg, and a sprinkle of smoked paprika.

Lunch:

- **Leftover Chicken Salad Wraps**
  Use leftover roasted chicken from Day 1, add a handful of greens, cucumbers, and a drizzle of yogurt dressing wrapped in a whole-wheat tortilla.

Dinner:

- **Lentil and Vegetable Soup**
  A hearty soup with lentils, carrots, celery, onions, garlic, and tomatoes. Serve with whole-grain bread for dipping.

DAY 3:

Breakfast:

- **Vegetable Omelet with Mushrooms, Bell Peppers, and Cheddar**
  Sauté mushrooms and bell peppers, then fold into a fluffy omelet with a bit of cheddar cheese. Serve with a side of sliced tomatoes.

Lunch:

- **Quinoa Salad with Roasted Vegetables and Lemon Dressing**
  Cook quinoa and toss with roasted vegetables (zucchini, bell peppers, and onions), a lemon vinaigrette, and a sprinkle of feta cheese.

Dinner:

- **Pan-Seared Salmon with Asparagus and Brown Rice**
  Season salmon fillets with lemon and dill, pan-sear until crispy, and serve with roasted asparagus and brown rice.

DAY 4:

Breakfast:

- **Avocado Toast with Egg and Sriracha**
  Top a slice of whole-grain toast with mashed avocado, a poached or fried egg, and a drizzle of sriracha for some heat.

Lunch:

- **Tuna Salad with Mixed Greens**
  Combine canned tuna (in olive oil) with chopped celery, onions, and a tablespoon of olive oil mayo. Serve over mixed greens with a lemon wedge.

Dinner:

- **Beef Stir-Fry with Vegetables and Rice**
  Stir-fry thinly sliced beef with garlic, ginger, and vegetables (carrots, bell peppers, broccoli). Serve over steamed white or brown rice.

DAY 5:

Breakfast:

- **Savory Greek Yogurt Bowl**
  Mix plain Greek yogurt with chopped cucumber, dill, garlic powder, and a drizzle of olive oil. Serve with a hard-boiled egg.

Lunch:

- **Leftover Beef Stir-Fry in Lettuce Wraps**
  Use leftover stir-fry from the night before. Wrap the mixture in large lettuce leaves for a light and crunchy lunch.

Dinner:

- **Baked Ziti with Spinach and Ricotta**
  Whole-wheat pasta tossed with marinara sauce, spinach, ricotta, and a sprinkle of parmesan cheese, baked until golden and bubbly.

DAY 6:

Breakfast:

- **Shakshuka**
  A savory dish of poached eggs in a tomato sauce with onions, garlic, and spices like cumin and paprika. Serve with whole-grain bread.

Lunch:

- **Chickpea and Avocado Salad**
  A simple salad with canned chickpeas, avocado, red onion, tomatoes, and a lemon-tahini dressing.

Dinner:

- **Grille Beef Chops with Roasted Brussels Sprouts and Mashed Potatoes**
  Grill beef chops and serve with roasted Brussels sprouts and mashed potatoes seasoned with garlic and olive oil.

DAY 7:

Breakfast:

- **Savory Breakfast Burrito**
  Scramble eggs with black beans, spinach, and a sprinkle of cheese. Wrap in a whole-wheat tortilla and top with salsa.

Lunch:

- **Leftover Grilled Pork Chop Salad**
  Use leftover pork from dinner to create a salad with mixed greens, roasted vegetables, and a mustard vinaigrette.

Dinner:

- **Vegetable and Tofu Stir-Fry**
  Stir-fry tofu with a mix of your favorite vegetables (broccoli, bell peppers, mushrooms) in soy sauce, sesame oil, and a touch of honey. Serve over quinoa or rice.

TIPS FOR THE MEAL PLAN:

- **Batch Cooking:** Prepare extra portions of grains (quinoa, rice) or roasted vegetables at the beginning of the week for easy assembly during busy days.
- **Leftovers:** Plan for leftovers to reduce cooking time and minimize waste—leftover protein (chicken, pork, beef) can be repurposed in salads or wraps.
- **Meal Prep:** You can prep vegetables for roasting or chopping ingredients ahead of time to make cooking quicker during the week.

This 7-day meal plan keeps things simple, balanced, and full of savory goodness to help you stay healthy, satisfied, and inspired in the kitchen!

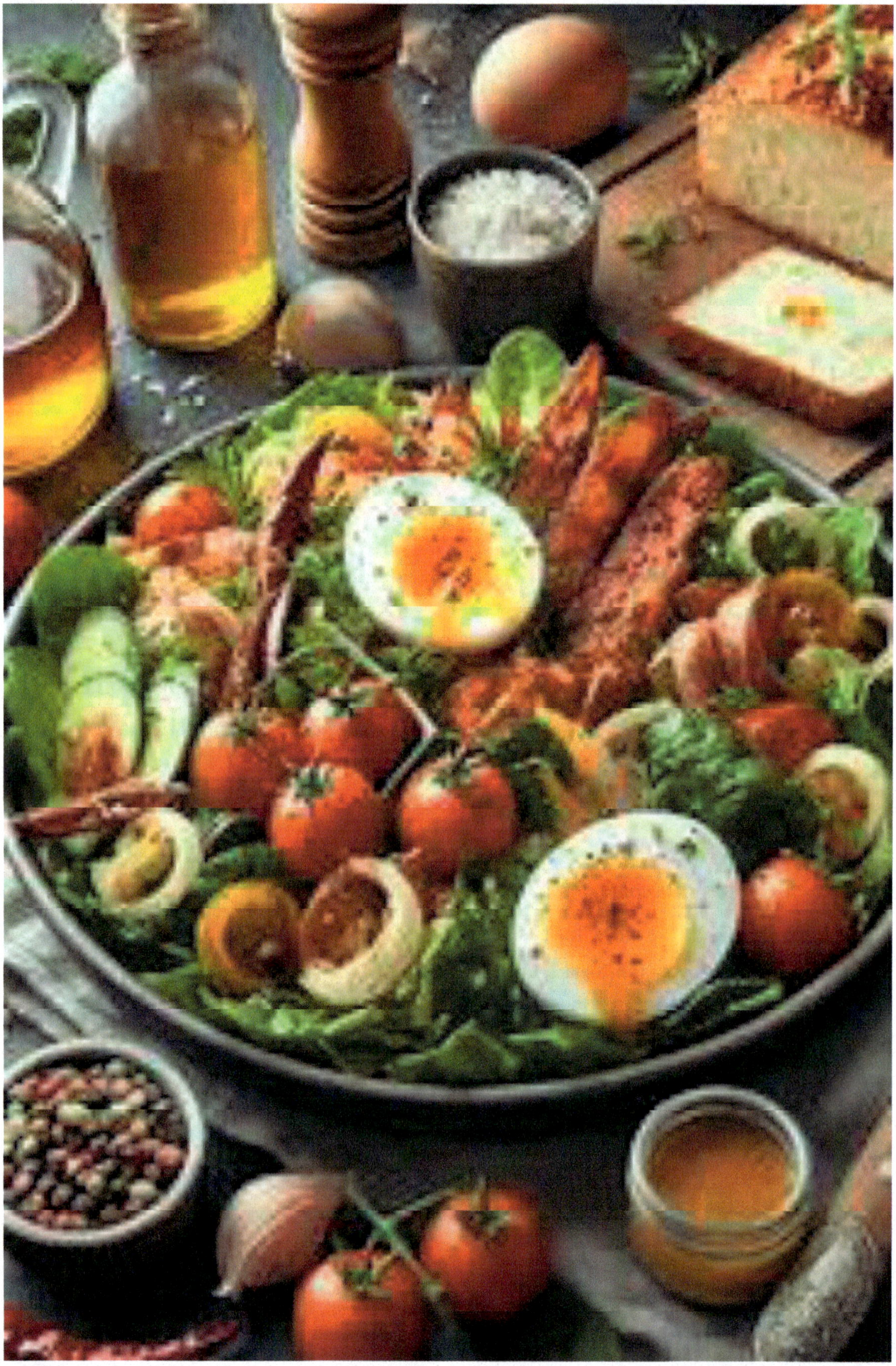

7 SAVORY BREAKFAST RECIPES

Here are seven savory breakfast recipes that are satisfying, flavorful, and packed with nutrients. Each recipe is easy to make, and I've included all the necessary details to help you get started.

SAVORY SCRAMBLED EGGS WITH SPINACH AND FETA

Ingredients:

- 2 large eggs
- 1/4 cup spinach, chopped
- 2 tbsp feta cheese, crumbled
- 1 tbsp olive oil or butter
- Salt and pepper to taste
- 1 slice whole-grain toast (optional)

Instructions:

1. Heat olive oil or butter in a pan over medium heat.
2. Add chopped spinach and sauté for 1-2 minutes until wilted.
3. Whisk eggs in a bowl, adding a pinch of salt and pepper.
4. Pour eggs into the pan with spinach and cook, stirring occasionally, until eggs are set (about 3-4 minutes).
5. Stir in crumbled feta cheese and cook for an additional minute.
6. Serve with a slice of whole-grain toast for added texture, if desired.

Cooking Time: 5 minutes
Prep Time: 2 minutes
Serving: 1
Nutritional Information (approx.):

- Calories: 290
- Protein: 18g
- Carbohydrates: 10g
- Fat: 22g
- Fiber: 3g

AVOCADO TOAST WITH EGG AND SRIRACHA

Ingredients:

- 1 slice whole-grain bread
- 1/2 avocado, mashed
- 1 large egg
- 1 tsp olive oil
- Sriracha sauce, to taste
- Salt and pepper to taste

Instructions:

1. Toast the slice of bread until golden brown.
2. In a small pan, heat olive oil over medium heat. Crack the egg into the pan and cook to your preferred doneness (sunny-side up or scrambled).
3. While the egg cooks, spread mashed avocado on the toasted bread.
4. Once the egg is cooked, place it on top of the avocado toast.
5. Drizzle with sriracha sauce, sprinkle with salt and pepper, and serve.

Cooking Time: 5 minutes
Prep Time: 2 minutes
Serving: 1
Nutritional Information (approx.):

- Calories: 350
- Protein: 12g
- Carbohydrates: 29g
- Fat: 22g
- Fiber: 10g

VEGETABLE OMELET WITH MUSHROOMS, BELL PEPPERS, AND CHEDDAR

Ingredients:

- 2 large eggs
- 1/4 cup mushrooms, sliced
- 1/4 cup bell pepper, diced
- 2 tbsp cheddar cheese, grated
- 1 tbsp olive oil or butter
- Salt and pepper to taste

Instructions:

1. Heat olive oil or butter in a skillet over medium heat.
2. Add sliced mushrooms and diced bell peppers. Cook for 3-4 minutes until softened.
3. Whisk eggs with salt and pepper, then pour over vegetables in the skillet.
4. Allow the eggs to cook for 2-3 minutes, then sprinkle cheddar cheese over the top.
5. Once the eggs are fully set, fold the omelet in half and serve.

Cooking Time: 5 minutes
Prep Time: 3 minutes
Serving: 1
Nutritional Information (approx.):

- Calories: 280
- Protein: 18g
- Carbohydrates: 7g
- Fat: 22g
- Fiber: 3g

SAVORY OATMEAL WITH AVOCADO AND POACHED EGG

Ingredients:

- 1/2 cup old-fashioned oats
- 1 cup low-sodium vegetable broth
- 1/2 avocado, sliced
- 1 large egg
- Salt and pepper to taste
- Red pepper flakes (optional)

Instructions:

1. In a saucepan, bring vegetable broth to a boil. Add oats, reduce the heat, and simmer for 5-7 minutes until the oats are soft and the liquid is absorbed.
2. While the oats cook, bring a pot of water to a gentle simmer. Crack the egg into a small cup and gently lower it into the water to poach for 3-4 minutes.
3. Once the oatmeal is cooked, transfer it to a bowl. Top with sliced avocado, poached egg, and a sprinkle of salt, pepper, and red pepper flakes.
4. Serve immediately.

Cooking Time: 10 minutes
Prep Time: 3 minutes
Serving: 1
Nutritional Information (approx.):

- Calories: 350
- Protein: 14g
- Carbohydrates: 35g
- Fat: 18g
- Fiber: 8g

SHAKSHUK (POACHED EGGS IN SPICY TOMATO SAUCE)

Ingredients:

- 1 tbsp olive oil
- 1/2 onion, chopped
- 1/2 bell pepper, diced
- 1 garlic clove, minced
- 1 can (14 oz) diced tomatoes
- 1 tsp cumin
- 1/2 tsp paprika
- 2 large eggs
- Salt and pepper to taste
- Fresh parsley for garnish

Instructions:

1. Heat olive oil in a skillet over medium heat. Add onions, bell pepper, and garlic. Cook until softened, about 5 minutes.
2. Add diced tomatoes, cumin, paprika, salt, and pepper. Simmer for 10 minutes until the sauce thickens.
3. Make two small wells in the sauce and crack an egg into each. Cover the skillet and cook for 5-7 minutes, until the eggs are poached to your liking.
4. Garnish with fresh parsley and serve with whole-grain bread for dipping.

Cooking Time: 15 minutes
Prep Time: 5 minutes
Serving: 2
Nutritional Information (approx. per serving):

- Calories: 280
- Protein: 14g
- Carbohydrates: 15g
- Fat: 18g
- Fiber: 5g

SAVORY BREAKFAST BURRITO

Ingredients:

- 1 large whole-wheat tortilla
- 2 large eggs
- 1/4 cup black beans, rinsed and drained
- 1/4 cup spinach, chopped
- 1/4 cup shredded cheese (cheddar or Mexican blend)
- Salsa, for topping
- Salt and pepper to taste

Instructions:

1. In a skillet, scramble eggs with salt and pepper. Add spinach and black beans to the eggs in the last minute of cooking.
2. Place the cooked mixture in the center of the tortilla, top with cheese, and fold the sides of the tortilla over the filling.
3. Roll the burrito tightly and heat it in the skillet for 2-3 minutes to brown the tortilla slightly.
4. Serve with salsa on the side.

Cooking Time: 5 minutes

Prep Time: 2 minutes

Serving: 1

Nutritional Information (approx.):

- Calories: 380
- Protein: 18g
- Carbohydrates: 35g
- Fat: 20g
- Fiber: 7g

EGG AND VEGGIE BREAKFAST BOWL

Ingredients:

- 2 large eggs
- 1/4 cup roasted sweet potato, cubed
- 1/4 cup sautéed kale or spinach
- 1 tbsp olive oil
- 1/4 avocado, sliced
- Hot sauce, to taste
- Salt and pepper to taste

Instructions:

1. In a skillet, cook the eggs to your liking (scrambled, fried, or poached).
2. While the eggs cook, sauté kale or spinach in olive oil until wilted.
3. In a bowl, layer the roasted sweet potato, sautéed greens, and cooked eggs.
4. Top with avocado slices, hot sauce, and a pinch of salt and pepper.

Cooking Time: 10 minutes
Prep Time: 3 minutes
Serving: 1
Nutritional Information (approx.):

- Calories: 380
- Protein: 14g
- Carbohydrates: 30g
- Fat: 24g
- Fiber: 8g

These savory breakfast recipes are packed with protein, healthy fats, and fiber to keep you energized and satisfied throughout the morning. Enjoy them as part of your balanced routine!

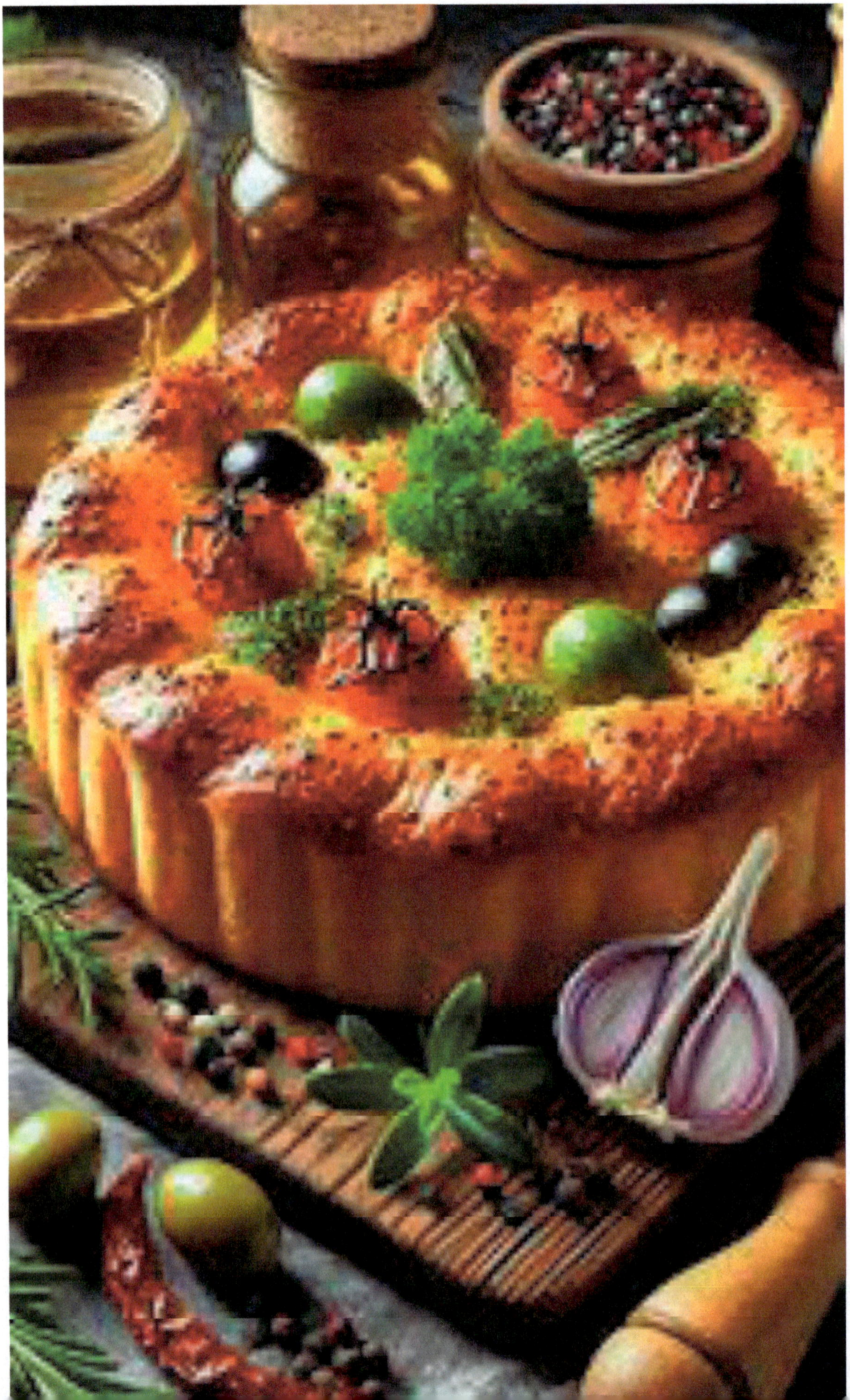

SAVORY LUNCH RECIPES

Here are seven savory lunch recipes that are flavorful, nutritious, and easy to prepare. Each recipe is designed to keep you satisfied while providing a healthy balance of protein, vegetables, and healthy fats.

GRILLED CHICKEN AND AVOCADO SALAD

Ingredients:

- 1 chicken breast (4-6 oz)
- 1 tbsp olive oil
- Salt and pepper to taste
- 2 cups mixed greens
- 1/2 avocado, sliced
- 1/4 cup cucumber, sliced
- 1/4 cup cherry tomatoes, halved
- 2 tbsp balsamic vinaigrette

Instructions:

1. Preheat the grill or a grill pan over medium heat.
2. Brush the chicken breast with olive oil and season with salt and pepper.
3. Grill the chicken for 6-7 minutes per side or until cooked through (internal temperature should reach 165°F/74°C).
4. Slice the grilled chicken into strips.
5. In a bowl, toss the mixed greens, avocado, cucumber, and cherry tomatoes.
6. Top with the grilled chicken and drizzle with balsamic vinaigrette.
7. Serve immediately.

Cooking Time: 15 minutes
Prep Time: 10 minutes
Serving: 1
Nutritional Information (approx.):

- Calories: 350
- Protein: 30g
- Carbohydrates: 12g
- Fat: 22g
- Fiber: 8g

QUINOA SALAD WITH ROASTED VEGETABLES AND LEMON DRESSING

Ingredients:

- 1/2 cup quinoa (uncooked)
- 1/2 cup bell peppers, diced
- 1/2 cup zucchini, diced
- 1/2 cup cherry tomatoes, halved
- 1 tbsp olive oil
- 1 tbsp lemon juice
- 1 tbsp fresh parsley, chopped
- Salt and pepper to taste

Instructions:

1. Preheat the oven to 400°F (200°C).
2. Toss the bell peppers, zucchini, and cherry tomatoes with olive oil, salt, and pepper.
3. Spread the vegetables on a baking sheet and roast for 20-25 minutes, until tender and lightly browned.
4. Meanwhile, cook the quinoa according to package instructions (usually about 15 minutes).
5. In a bowl, combine the cooked quinoa, roasted vegetables, and fresh parsley.
6. Drizzle with lemon juice and toss gently.
7. Serve warm or chilled.

Cooking Time: 30 minutes
Prep Time: 10 minutes
Serving: 2
Nutritional Information (approx. per serving):

- Calories: 320
- Protein: 8g
- Carbohydrates: 40g
- Fat: 14g
- Fiber: 6g

LENTIL SOUP WITH CARROTS AND CELERY

Ingredients:

- 1 cup dried lentils, rinsed
- 1 tbsp olive oil
- 1 small onion, chopped
- 2 garlic cloves, minced
- 2 carrots, diced
- 2 celery stalks, diced
- 1 can (14.5 oz) diced tomatoes
- 4 cups vegetable broth
- 1 tsp cumin
- Salt and pepper to taste
- Fresh parsley for garnish

Instructions:

1. In a large pot, heat olive oil over medium heat. Add onion and garlic, sautéing for 2-3 minutes until softened.
2. Add carrots, celery, cumin, salt, and pepper. Stir and cook for 5 minutes.
3. Pour in the diced tomatoes and vegetable broth. Bring to a simmer.
4. Add the lentils and cook for 25-30 minutes, until lentils are tender.
5. Adjust seasoning with salt and pepper to taste.
6. Serve with fresh parsley as garnish.

Cooking Time: 35 minutes
Prep Time: 10 minutes
Serving: 4
Nutritional Information (approx. per serving):

- Calories: 210
- Protein: 12g
- Carbohydrates: 38g
- Fat: 3g
- Fiber: 14g

TURKEY AND AVOCADO LETTUCE WRAPS

Ingredients:

- 4 slices turkey breast (deli meat, nitrate-free)
- 1/2 avocado, sliced
- 1/4 cup cucumber, sliced
- 1/4 cup shredded carrots
- 2 large Romaine lettuce leaves
- 1 tbsp hummus (optional)
- Salt and pepper to taste

Instructions:

1. Lay out the lettuce leaves and spread a thin layer of hummus (optional).
2. On each lettuce leaf, place 2 slices of turkey, avocado slices, cucumber, and shredded carrots.
3. Season with salt and pepper.
4. Roll up the lettuce leaves like a burrito and serve immediately.

Cooking Time: 5 minutes
Prep Time: 5 minutes
Serving: 2
Nutritional Information (approx. per serving):

- Calories: 250
- Protein: 20g
- Carbohydrates: 12g
- Fat: 18g
- Fiber: 8g

SALMON AND ROASTED BRUSSELS SPROUTS SALAD

Ingredients:

- 1 salmon fillet (4-6 oz)
- 1 tbsp olive oil
- Salt and pepper to taste
- 1 cup Brussels sprouts, halved
- 2 cups mixed greens
- 1 tbsp balsamic vinaigrette
- 1 tbsp sunflower seeds (optional)

Instructions:

1. Preheat the oven to 400°F (200°C).
2. Season the salmon fillet with olive oil, salt, and pepper. Place it on a baking sheet.
3. Toss the Brussels sprouts with olive oil, salt, and pepper, then spread them on the same baking sheet as the salmon.
4. Roast for 15-20 minutes, until the salmon is cooked through (internal temperature should reach 145°F/63°C) and the Brussels sprouts are crispy.
5. Assemble the salad by placing mixed greens in a bowl and topping with roasted Brussels sprouts, the baked salmon, and sunflower seeds.
6. Drizzle with balsamic vinaigrette and serve.

Cooking Time: 20 minutes
Prep Time: 10 minutes
Serving: 1
Nutritional Information (approx.):

- Calories: 450
- Protein: 30g
- Carbohydrates: 18g
- Fat: 30g
- Fiber: 9g

CHICKPEA AND TOMATO STEW

Ingredients:

- 1 can (15 oz) chickpeas, drained and rinsed
- 1 can (14.5 oz) diced tomatoes
- 1 small onion, chopped
- 2 garlic cloves, minced
- 1 tsp cumin
- 1/2 tsp paprika
- 1/2 cup vegetable broth
- 1 tbsp olive oil
- Salt and pepper to taste
- Fresh cilantro for garnish

Instructions:

1. In a large pot, heat olive oil over medium heat. Add onion and garlic, sautéing for 3 minutes until softened.
2. Add cumin, paprika, salt, and pepper. Stir and cook for 1 minute.
3. Add chickpeas, diced tomatoes, and vegetable broth. Bring to a simmer.
4. Cook for 15-20 minutes, stirring occasionally, until the stew thickens slightly.
5. Garnish with fresh cilantro and serve.

Cooking Time: 25 minutes
Prep Time: 5 minutes
Serving: 2
Nutritional Information (approx. per serving):

- Calories: 320
- Protein: 14g
- Carbohydrates: 45g
- Fat: 10g
- Fiber: 12g

EGG SALAD WITH ROASTED SWEET POTATOES

Ingredients:

- 2 hard-boiled eggs, chopped
- 1 small sweet potato, diced
- 1 tbsp olive oil
- 1 tbsp Greek yogurt
- 1 tsp Dijon mustard
- Salt and pepper to taste
- Fresh parsley for garnish

Instructions:

1. Preheat the oven to 400°F (200°C). Toss diced sweet potato with olive oil, salt, and pepper. Roast on a baking sheet for 20 minutes, or until tender.
2. In a bowl, combine the chopped hard-boiled eggs, Greek yogurt, Dijon mustard, salt, and pepper.
3. Once the sweet potatoes are roasted, add them to the egg salad mixture.
4. Garnish with fresh parsley and serve.

Cooking Time: 25 minutes
Prep Time: 5 minutes
Serving: 1
Nutritional Information (approx.):

- Calories: 350
- Protein: 18g
- Carbohydrates: 40g
- Fat: 14g
- Fiber: 8g

These savory lunch recipes are simple, filling, and packed with flavor. Each recipe is designed to be balanced and nutritious, giving you plenty of energy to power through your day!

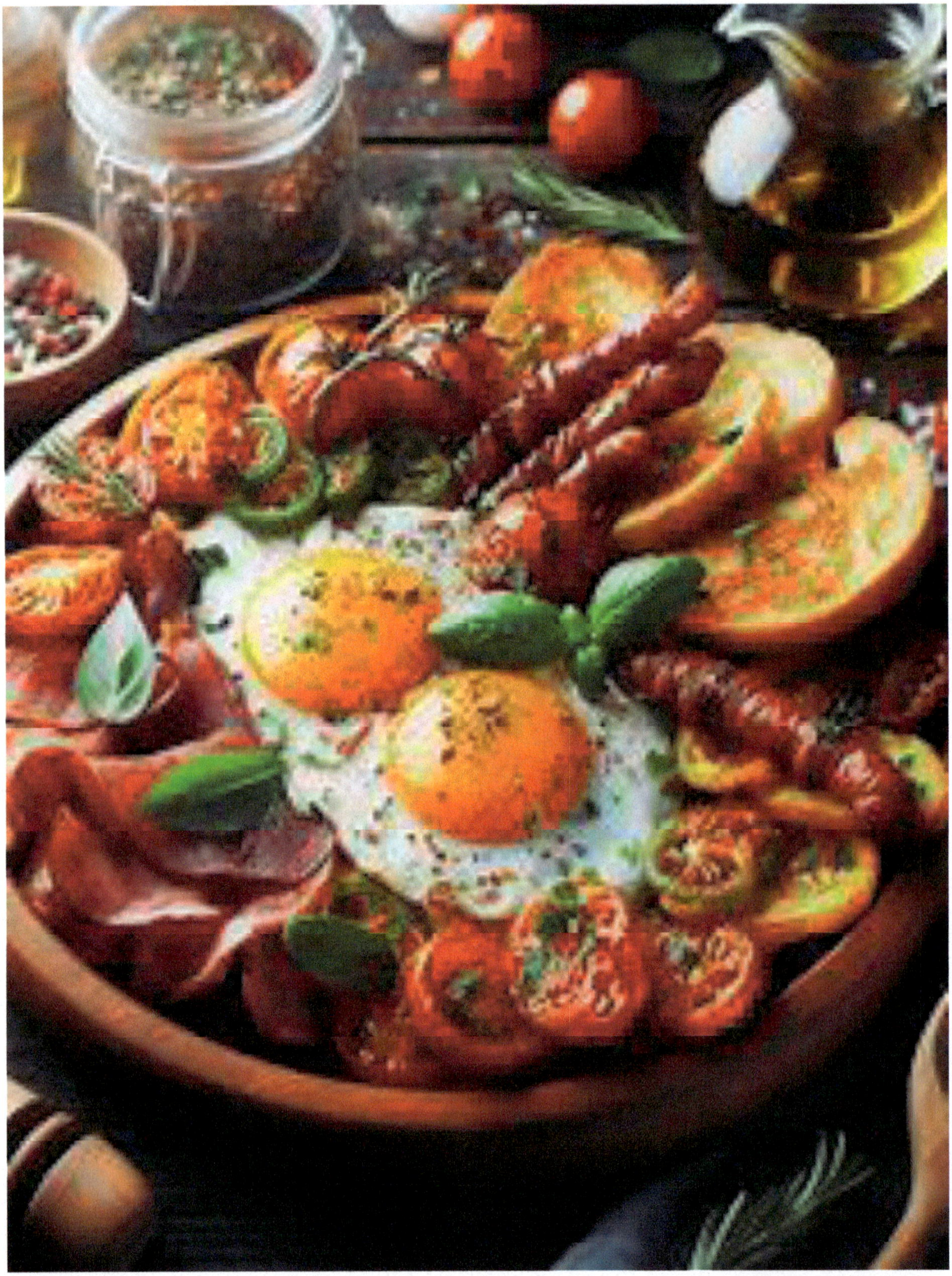

SAVORY DINNER RECIPES

Here are seven savory dinner recipes that are hearty, nutritious, and packed with flavor. Each recipe is designed to be easy to prepare and perfect for a satisfying evening meal.

GARLIC BUTTER SHRIMP AND ASPARAGUS

Ingredients:

- 1 lb shrimp, peeled and deveined
- 1 bunch asparagus, trimmed and cut into 2-inch pieces
- 3 tbsp butter
- 4 garlic cloves, minced
- 1 tbsp lemon juice
- Salt and pepper to taste
- 1 tbsp fresh parsley, chopped

Instructions:

1. Heat 1 tablespoon of butter in a large skillet over medium heat. Add asparagus and cook for 4-5 minutes until tender but still crisp. Remove and set aside.
2. In the same skillet, melt the remaining butter. Add garlic and sauté for 1-2 minutes until fragrant.
3. Add shrimp to the skillet and cook for 2-3 minutes per side until pink and opaque.
4. Stir in lemon juice, salt, and pepper. Add the cooked asparagus back into the skillet.
5. Toss to combine, then garnish with fresh parsley.
6. Serve immediately.

Cooking Time: 10 minutes
Prep Time: 5 minutes
Serving: 2
Nutritional Information (approx. per serving):

- Calories: 350
- Protein: 40g
- Carbohydrates: 10g
- Fat: 18g
- Fiber: 4g

BAKED LEMON HERB CHICKEN THIGHS

Ingredients:

- 4 bone-in, skin-on chicken thighs
- 2 tbsp olive oil
- 1 tbsp lemon zest
- 2 tbsp lemon juice
- 1 tsp garlic powder
- 1 tsp dried thyme
- 1 tsp dried rosemary
- Salt and pepper to taste

Instructions:

1. Preheat the oven to 400°F (200°C).
2. In a small bowl, mix olive oil, lemon zest, lemon juice, garlic powder, thyme, rosemary, salt, and pepper.
3. Rub the mixture all over the chicken thighs.
4. Place the chicken thighs on a baking sheet, skin side up.
5. Bake for 35-40 minutes or until the chicken reaches an internal temperature of 165°F (74°C) and the skin is crispy.
6. Serve with your favorite side dish.

Cooking Time: 40 minutes
Prep Time: 10 minutes
Serving: 4
Nutritional Information (approx. per serving):

- Calories: 380
- Protein: 30g
- Carbohydrates: 4g
- Fat: 28g
- Fiber: 1g

SPAGHETTI SQUASH WITH MARINARA SAUCE AND TURKEY MEATBALLS

Ingredients:

- 1 medium spaghetti squash
- 1 lb ground turkey
- 1 egg
- 1/4 cup breadcrumbs
- 1/4 cup grated Parmesan cheese
- 1 tsp Italian seasoning
- 1 jar marinara sauce (about 24 oz)
- Salt and pepper to taste

Instructions:

1. Preheat the oven to 400°F (200°C).
2. Slice the spaghetti squash in half lengthwise and scoop out the seeds. Place the halves cut side down on a baking sheet and bake for 35-40 minutes until tender.
3. While the squash bakes, mix the ground turkey, egg, breadcrumbs, Parmesan cheese, Italian seasoning, salt, and pepper in a bowl.
4. Form the mixture into meatballs and place them on a baking sheet. Bake for 20-25 minutes until fully cooked (internal temperature should reach 165°F/74°C).
5. In a saucepan, heat the marinara sauce over medium heat. Add the cooked meatballs and simmer for 5 minutes.
6. Once the squash is done, use a fork to scrape the flesh into spaghetti-like strands.
7. Serve the meatballs and marinara sauce over the spaghetti squash.

Cooking Time: 45 minutes
Prep Time: 10 minutes
Serving: 4
Nutritional Information (approx. per serving):

- Calories: 320
- Protein: 30g
- Carbohydrates: 16g
- Fat: 18g
- Fiber: 6g

BEEF STIR-FRY WITH VEGETABLES

Ingredients:

- 1 lb beef sirloin, thinly sliced
- 1 tbsp sesame oil
- 1 red bell pepper, thinly sliced
- 1 yellow bell pepper, thinly sliced
- 1 zucchini, sliced
- 1/2 cup broccoli florets
- 3 tbsp soy sauce (or tamari for gluten-free)
- 1 tbsp rice vinegar
- 1 tsp grated ginger
- 2 garlic cloves, minced
- 2 tbsp green onions, sliced

Instructions:

1. Heat sesame oil in a large skillet or wok over medium-high heat.
2. Add the sliced beef and stir-fry for 2-3 minutes until browned. Remove the beef and set aside.
3. In the same skillet, add the bell peppers, zucchini, and broccoli. Stir-fry for 4-5 minutes until the vegetables are tender-crisp.
4. Add garlic and ginger and cook for an additional minute.
5. Return the beef to the skillet and stir in soy sauce, rice vinegar, and green onions.
6. Cook for 2-3 minutes until the beef is cooked through and the sauce has thickened.
7. Serve immediately.

Cooking Time: 10 minutes
Prep Time: 5 minutes
Serving: 4
Nutritional Information (approx. per serving):

- Calories: 280
- Protein: 30g
- Carbohydrates: 14g
- Fat: 14g
- Fiber: 5g

STUFFED BELL PEPPERS WITH QUINOA AND GROUND BEEF

Ingredients:

- 4 large bell peppers
- 1 lb ground beef
- 1/2 cup cooked quinoa
- 1 small onion, chopped
- 2 garlic cloves, minced
- 1 can (14.5 oz) diced tomatoes
- 1 tsp cumin
- 1/2 tsp chili powder
- 1/4 cup shredded cheese (optional)
- Salt and pepper to taste

Instructions:

1. Preheat the oven to 375°F (190°C).
2. Cut the tops off the bell peppers and remove the seeds. Place them in a baking dish.
3. In a skillet, cook the ground beef over medium heat until browned.
4. Add the chopped onion and garlic, cooking for 2-3 minutes until softened.
5. Stir in the cooked quinoa, diced tomatoes, cumin, chili powder, salt, and pepper. Cook for 5 minutes until well combined.
6. Stuff the bell peppers with the beef and quinoa mixture.
7. Cover the baking dish with foil and bake for 25 minutes. If desired, top with shredded cheese and bake uncovered for an additional 5 minutes.
8. Serve immediately.

Cooking Time: 35 minutes
Prep Time: 10 minutes
Serving: 4
Nutritional Information (approx. per serving):

- Calories: 330
- Protein: 30g
- Carbohydrates: 25g
- Fat: 18g
- Fiber: 6g

BEEF TENDERLOIN WITH ROASTED ROOT VEGETABLES

Ingredients:

- 1 lb beef tenderloin
- 2 tbsp olive oil
- 2 large carrots, peeled and cut into chunks
- 1 parsnip, peeled and cut into chunks
- 1 medium sweet potato, peeled and cut into chunks
- 1 tsp dried thyme
- 1 tsp garlic powder
- Salt and pepper to taste

Instructions:

1. Preheat the oven to 400°F (200°C).
2. Season the beef tenderloin with olive oil, salt, pepper, thyme, and garlic powder.
3. Place the beef tenderloin on a baking sheet. Surround it with the carrots, parsnips, and sweet potatoes.
4. Roast for 25-30 minutes, or until the beef reaches an internal temperature of 145°F (63°C) and the vegetables are tender.
5. Let the beef rest for 5 minutes before slicing.
6. Serve the sliced pork with roasted root vegetables.

Cooking Time: 35 minutes
Prep Time: 10 minutes
Serving: 4
Nutritional Information (approx. per serving):

- Calories: 400
- Protein: 30g
- Carbohydrates: 35g
- Fat: 18g
- Fiber: 8g

VEGETARIAN CHILI

Ingredients:

- 1 tbsp olive oil
- 1 onion, chopped
- 2 garlic cloves, minced
- 1 can (15 oz) black beans, drained and rinsed
- 1 can (15 oz) kidney beans, drained and rinsed
- 1 can (14.5 oz) diced tomatoes
- 1 cup corn kernels
- 1 tsp chili powder
- 1/2 tsp cumin
- 1/2 tsp smoked paprika
- Salt and pepper to taste
- Fresh cilantro for garnish

Instructions:

1. In a large pot, heat olive oil over medium heat. Add onion and garlic and sauté for 3 minutes until softened.
2. Add the black beans, kidney beans, diced tomatoes, corn, chili powder, cumin, smoked paprika, salt, and pepper. Stir to combine.
3. Bring the chili to a simmer and cook for 20-25 minutes, stirring occasionally.
4. Adjust seasoning with salt and pepper.
5. Serve the chili garnished with fresh cilantro.

Cooking Time: 30 minutes
Prep Time: 10 minutes
Serving: 4
Nutritional Information (approx. per serving):

- Calories: 280
- Protein: 12g
- Carbohydrates: 45g
- Fat: 7g
- Fiber: 15g

These savory dinner recipes are simple, filling, and full of nutrients to keep you energized throughout the evening. Each meal offers a variety of flavors and textures to suit different tastes!

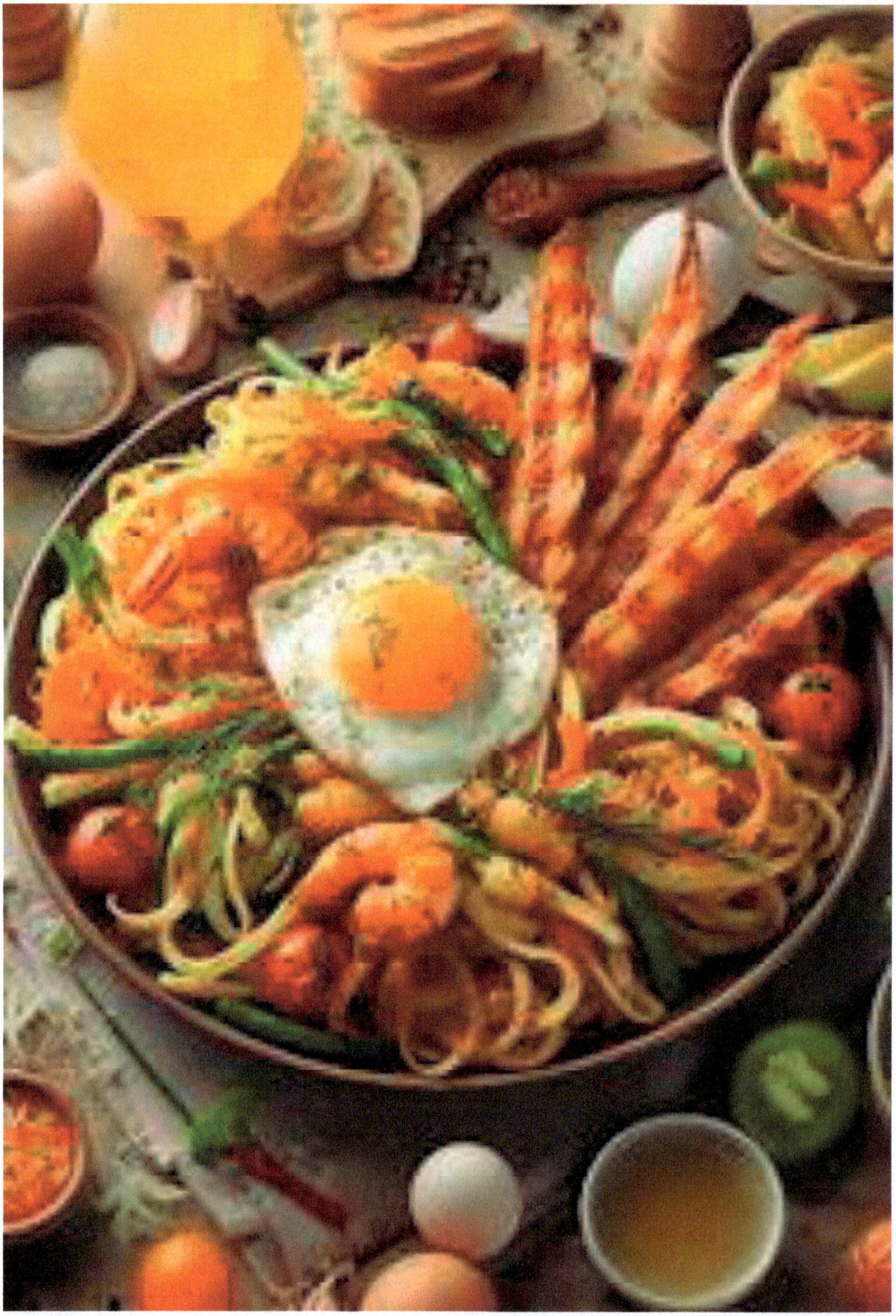

CONCLUSION

As we reach the end of our savory journey together in *THE SAVORY & SIMPLE KITCHEN*, I hope you've found inspiration and confidence in the recipes and techniques that have been shared. This cookbook was designed not only to teach you the art of savory cooking but also to bring the joy and ease of preparing simple, delicious, and nutritious meals into your daily routine.

The savory recipes in this book are meant to show you that great cooking doesn't have to be complicated—it's about balance, flavor, and embracing the ingredients that bring comfort and satisfaction to every dish. Whether it's a quick breakfast to start your day, a nourishing lunch to power through the afternoon, or a fulfilling dinner to wrap up your evening, these recipes have been curated to ensure that you can enjoy the richness of savory flavors without the stress of intricate techniques or hours of preparation.

Remember, cooking is as much about the experience as it is about the outcome. It's about the joy of transforming fresh, simple ingredients into dishes that nurture and delight. As you continue your cooking journey, allow yourself the freedom to experiment with flavors, textures, and ingredients, while remembering that the key to savory cooking lies in consistency and a few tried-and-true principles.

Whether you are new to savory cooking or looking to refine your skills, *THE SAVORY & SIMPLE KITCHEN* offers a space where both beginners and seasoned cooks can learn, grow, and savor the process of creating meals that nourish the body and soul.

Thank you for taking the time to explore these recipes and techniques. I encourage you to continue filling your kitchen with the aromas of savory dishes and to savor each moment spent preparing and sharing meals with those you care about. Keep it simple, keep it savory, and always remember that the best meals are those made with love and passion.

Happy cooking!

WEEKLY PLANNER

Fighting!

MONTH: **WEEK OF:**

MONDAY

TUESDAY

WEDNESDAY

THURSDAY

FRIDAY

SATURDAY

SUNDAY

NOTE:

WEEKLY PLANNER

Fighting!

MONTH: **WEEK OF:**

MONDAY	TUESDAY	WEDNESDAY

THURSDAY	FRIDAY	SATURDAY

SUNDAY

NOTE:

WEEKLY PLANNER

Fighting!

MONTH: **WEEK OF:**

MONDAY	TUESDAY	WEDNESDAY

THURSDAY	FRIDAY	SATURDAY

SUNDAY	NOTE:

WEEKLY PLANNER

Fighting!

MONTH: **WEEK OF:**

MONDAY

TUESDAY

WEDNESDAY

THURSDAY

FRIDAY

SATURDAY

SUNDAY

NOTE:

WEEKLY PLANNER

Fighting!

MONTH: **WEEK OF:**

MONDAY

TUESDAY

WEDNESDAY

THURSDAY

FRIDAY

SATURDAY

SUNDAY

NOTE:

WEEKLY PLANNER

Fighting!

MONTH: **WEEK OF:**

MONDAY	TUESDAY	WEDNESDAY

THURSDAY	FRIDAY	SATURDAY

SUNDAY	NOTE:

WEEKLY PLANNER

Fighting!

MONTH:　　**WEEK OF:**

MONDAY	TUESDAY	WEDNESDAY

THURSDAY	FRIDAY	SATURDAY

SUNDAY	NOTE:

WEEKLY PLANNER

Fighting!

MONTH: **WEEK OF:**

MONDAY

TUESDAY

WEDNESDAY

THURSDAY

FRIDAY

SATURDAY

SUNDAY

NOTE:

WEEKLY PLANNER

Fighting!

MONTH: **WEEK OF:**

MONDAY

TUESDAY

WEDNESDAY

THURSDAY

FRIDAY

SATURDAY

SUNDAY

NOTE:

WEEKLY PLANNER

Fighting!

MONTH: **WEEK OF:**

MONDAY

TUESDAY

WEDNESDAY

THURSDAY

FRIDAY

SATURDAY

SUNDAY

NOTE:

Printed in Great Britain
by Amazon